Uncommon
Grammar
Cloth

Uncommon Grammar Cloth

Cheryl Pallant

STATION HILL
BARRYTOWN, LTD.

Published by Station Hill / Barrytown, Ltd. in Barrytown, New York 12507.

E-mail: publishers@stationhill.org
Online catalogue: http://www.stationhill.org

Station Hill Arts is a project of The Institute for Publishing Arts, Inc., a not-for-profit, federally tax exempt organization in Barrytown, New York, which gratefully acknowledges ongoing support for its publishing program from the New York State Council on the Arts.

A number of the works in this collection have been published in the following journals: *Coe Review, Dirigible, Empty Set, Lyric, New York Quarterly,* and *proximity.*

Cover design by Kevin Heffernan with assistance from Susan Quasha.

Library of Congress Cataloging-in-Publication Data

Pallant, Cheryl.
  Uncommon grammar cloth / Cheryl Pallant.
    p. cm.
  ISBN 1-58177-080-4 (alk. paper)
    I. Title
  PS3566.A4637 U54 2001
  811'.54—dc21   00-067477

Manufactured in The United States of America

Acknowledgments

The author would like to express gratitude to Lisa Willow, Grant Jenkins, Lenore Gay, Lisa Schiffer, Kevin Heffernan, and my many dance partners who set my words in motion.

We usually evaluate creative process in terms of how much feeling or thinking was behind the work or how well the work was done. Is there any other way of appreciating the process? What if the standard of excellence was how fully present the artist was during the process?

Kazuaki Tanahashi

Let yourself go, let the writing flow, let yourself steep; bathe, relax, become the river, let everything go, open up, unwind, open the floodgates, let yourself roll...A practice of greatest passivity...This mode of passivity is our way—really an active way—of getting to know things by letting ourselves be known by them.

Hélène Cixous

Syntax is a faculty of the soul.

Paul Valéry

1

she who hesitates is not necessarily lost but has
found a new way or is looking to get off the one
way ramp leading to the large car lot of carnivorous
pleasures carnivaling senses unlike anything known
before, like something outside her neighborhood,
like some place she would never walk her dog or
garage her park.

she who hesitates is not necessarily lost but has
found is finding a new way different from the cold
way, searching for the link. she who is hesitant has
not necessarily been this way before, pinned there
done that, perhaps stumbling because of awkward
fitting shoes that crush toes and misstep everywhere
she goes and is going to change what pains her if she
can determine cause, or the heck with historical
causes, she's living for the moment, for the week-
end, for the weak kneed who once upon delighted
now give cause to barf, excuse me for living, no

excuses for she who struts her stuffing it down the turkey's gullet, ensuring juiciness despite using store bought brands or making crumbs from scratching her back room sale that few get to see, fewer still invited because they rummage through the racks with attitudes bigger than boss me around.

this hesitating character i know well, recently acquainted the other day when in a store of surprises, colors beyond the daily gross national product which is what kept me enthralled, that and the blare of music that shivered my spine, shivered me timbers, lighting a small fire of inspiration to buy what i normally would not, to try on whimsy, nothing more, nothing less expensive, i wanted something less expensive, these the concerns of the underemployed, underestimated, and under wearing out and stopping for something more practical, is there anything less practical than this, i thought, which is precisely what caught my fanciful eye, a fantasy not yet explored, kept hideously cornered, born for another age, i'm aging so fast to slow down my desires and examinations were never my strength, standardized tests and such, but this question had me stumped, like so many others, different with its blaze of color, its quite contrariness, can we loop the spool to lead elsewhere, i kept coming back despite my leaving behind.

i walked away my purchase unpurchased but too late, it already seeded my mind, perverted my privacy code broken into, raked into bits, but i did walk away and carry on with daily doings increasingly undone, increasingly thinking about what gets left behind because hesitation ceased control of ecstatic fantasy yearnings so impractical to want them everyday in any way, a trespass into barbed yards and barn yards where pigs squeal and goats jump to instincts' delight while i tell another story, while i distrust urging me on, goading me on and on about how necessary this inessential item, okay, only twenty dollars, only twenty, i can come up with that, can't i welcome what toys between floored and shelved, something i can wear and flare to my heart's delight, forget about mindreason drifting off, sleep away, stored away, there's got to be purpose if only a whim.

so the other day i called my friend, left a message of buy it for me, must buy it form me in the way i want, in the way i don't know about me, you claim to know more about me than i do not listen to what you say i'm hearing another voice, cross current, party line, marxist uprising that taunts me time to time for a change, this inexplicable unreasoned permit me to not excuse myself to be a must of my former self emerging like fined for not conforming to the seed of your mustard but to the well of my own deep, craving for the loop-de-loo, and off with your head, your reason doesn't fit here, try on this shoe. i'm not cinderella, more the rakish type who would rather run off in the woods to chant than sit behind the wheel trafficking your desires.

into the bowels of earth, ancient stirrings call
waiting call forth. earth bowels moving van
winkler. earthen yowls and shouts labor of misgiv-
ings, back hoes scrape skin, removing tree debris.
ancient ear rings, call to a voice faintly familiar,
faintly urging, fainting into the arms of amour,
wanting more of what's at seed. sectionally divided,
i am model homed, shopping complexed, yearning
for the sprawl of field desert tundra jungle wood
ocean where i dip as please, float in the apple of
eyeing the expanse uninterrupted, lose myself,
loosen the ropes of discord, me apart from your
shrine, your pain apart from the flame blazing in
me.

so separate, so cubicled in our limbic tangle, tan-
gentially relating through civic pride, a finger
pointing out or up yours. i walk with hands pock-
eted, my strands striating from the ground of my
desiring for all us a sun in belly up, a bally-hoo, a
hidee-ho. (chorus, chime in, please.)

so many have forgotten though we've daily remind-
ers: the blink of the switchboard requesting a
switching of channels, a washing fully behind the ear
rings again, reminder that someone is talking about,
someone is balking, someone is blaming another for
our demise. and it's not that i know better than you
know better whether to batter with butter or switch
hit the knitter. it's not its snot that i'm avoiding my
own role in what's the matter with me, matter

matter face on fire and such as like but simply inconsequentially and sequentially is what i'm limited to, one foot in front of the other, one step on my foot, if you do, i'll switch hit that nosing into my business. (chorus, chant as please.)

at root, fully in the duodenum of the matter passing through sometimes too fast or slow and sometimes not at all call the doctor. at root is an evolution that few can conceive, let alone, leave me alone, everybody share, be nice while planetary urgings shower rain and glee, a volcanic spew charring not only civic pride, but every bit our toys, computers, four wheel drive vehicles racing nowhere, the terrain of past buried, the terrain of future so modified as to forget the flesh skin skein of cave dwelling.

only get pissed off in the pissed ·off hour or at the function therapeutically designed to modify qualities careful within reason lie on the couch, would you sign your checking in with how you're doing all the wrong things, too much righteousness, having forgotten mammalian urges, the soft fur of desire this moment a sun, a pounce, a perch in a high palm tree and swing from arm to arm without arms race and ample space to tail our limbs, tell our tales, and listen to the stars shine their distant beach.

she and he come together. she and he c-come, but too quickly we rapid role hollywood style for profit, all ways for profit, the ultimate ferengi way which on tv we laugh at and chuckle tee-hee, recognizing ourselves but without image rooting deeply enough for matter to rematter into mythic remaking, a mistful revolution of turning our gaze to the horizon viewable not via plugged device but while sitting on the ridge at the ocean of the mountains in the desert of our soul contained yet uncontainable which is why we sit together apart, live in our bodies but aren't home and i've had just about enough and want to uncome myself, the final brigade, a final combing through my own tangle yours. (chorus, drift off, please.)

3

bones invite wind to stir ancestral longings, ply this flesh, squeeze impurities out. wind invites bones to ancestral longings while daze holds me apart, threatening me to away with watchfulness, to sink release into indefinable current, to let go. always such resistance while yearning. always such yearning in resist. body mind emotion spirit confer at the table appropriating time. balance the ballast, she's gonna blow. they pour more coffee. call in the reinforcements. order some pizza. this over-whelmed body weeps in the torrent of the ages.

she can do it another way, elbows one in the shad-ows.

she summons shadows to her office. when they fail to show, she retreats to the woods, hears their approach, though no figures show, only their estimation, only their liminal selves. she accepts the terms of their presence, asks for new terms to define herself. they suggest none, only feel, root, soften, allow creamsicle afternoons and palatial mornings, faxing in the night. she drifts up to tree tops and they pull her to the sky, rooting her on. she obliges her hunger, ancient ache, and strips off her skin. naked as wind, sun, and soar, easily blended, borrowed, gone everywhere present, tongue of flame, elbowing cliffs, a fountaining of senselessness, thingless and thankful. swans drift down river, bees hover, clouds climb mountains, cascading into billow. coreless to the core, she walks away returned.

4

continually they ask me. containfully they put nothing as question, more supposition, that i abide by their rules, put blocks in holes, yet my circles don't fit. they force the point though limited geometry lessons show that unless the holes break, or i do, that the fit will not.

st-steam release. ac-acumen. brrr-ristle. mary has little lambs, cramps run down my legs. in the freeze dried brain slump sequestering i from you, my yolk seeps through the shell. so fertile, we, yet do nothing. so wormy. i take it upon myself this leaden weight that leads me to us to ride the bus, waves, echoes of accordions, tablas, chimes, my dna remembering another continent, this american home baffling me with its decree to mall myself. where is a-cept a-cept accents. when your corn is monkey and i refuse to feast. thank you, not hungry at the moment. thank you, i'll take a rain checking me out the door. thank you, jungle calling. away from architectured constructs. away from plastic wrap. away from credit cartography. i am hemispherically challenged.

the grass is greener, a penny saved, stitches in lime. i wear an uncommon grammar cloth to hip my sway, nerve spine with snake uncoiled pursuing heat, always heat, skin, blood, come to the other side to dreaming fields, the feel of footed flight and wings of utmost desire. left behind before, i cannot leave behind again. i do this all for you, my synonymous, because no other words suffice.

hopelessly writing the body, sometimes as my hand sifting your flesh, willing what i may, will-less as the sun's rise and fall and up again. listen to the advice of wind, rice, and baaaaffles. quietly in their iridescent skitter, geckoes enter hut, pose, and transpose. we are never the same again.

continually the moment invents me, invests me with faith battle doubt my own falls and rises, irises and corneated aster risking. bloom and fold, bloom and i told you not to go there you are gaining on me. we are not so separate as you think about it gaining on you, raining on you, summering in your winter. widen your whole, soften your block, often. set aside, sit down, float in your craft and do not force issuing me standard uniforms, however

8

well starched and folded against breath. ether your oxygen and ex-ex-ex-hale spansively and realize that all i ever do is pray in our behalf be whole.

5

writing is a gesture of love and i am hopelessly fallen in. i know no other way out there on the fringe of social instability, laddering thoughts to the moon. we collaborate secretly in the tree house. we corroborate breath with every shirt and tuck. my failure is in doing, undone because be. a failure yet believe me you when the heat stream billows little matters but utterances rinsing. gesture my only hope. gesture my only nope you don't easily see me through your fog. but it's not even about hope. not even. maybe faith but not even. oddly enough, odd enough is enough while never is always. twisting like a chorded rope, irresistible twine.

nothing is beneath me nor above my synonymous. i am fed eponyms and eat with innards in tact fully. in reprieve from. drawing up sleeves. pulling at thread baring all. staring at shouldn't yet do any and all, the ins and outs, ifs and whenever to please ease dis-comfort. too often i have upped the hill down, ragged riches, and amped doubt. breath devours me and i lose myself to weeding through the high grasses skinless.

do not think of me do not think. words express train with no known e.t.a. b.r.q. l-m-n-o-p. reme-

dial tuning inward, switched on and into bigger and
better. hopelessly without, i have fallen for inflec-
tions. allow me, at least, to punctuate.

6

i can never return. i am waiting to arrive. i'm not
sending myself off and on, switched in the up or
down, following pursuit, wearing jeans, typically,
asymptomatically, lustering after that which hovers
on outskirts hemming me in. i follow threads and
tangle with gnarls, the nature of substance, i sup-
pose, the nature of delicate material, i suppose, and
try to forget, try to flatten understanding under a
pile of books. i crave returning to arrive. *arrivedirci*,
mi amigo. i mix cultures into a semi-sweet yogurt of
my dreaming. the want to arrive gets blocks by
want without flashing light my way around possible
crash. blocked and blue, my slowness, too, hinders
spindles from spinning. my navigational skills are
off, land where there should be none, wave where
there might be cresting possibilities or a shawl
draped over the shouldering of burdens. feet tap
impatience yet this patina, too, blocks yet blues.

a more aerial sort, with capes perhaps, would leap
in faith, would steep not in knowledge but sensation
of wind breeze survival rests in landing not with
head but feet. i wait with bated breath. i wait with
steeped head. unknittingly, i snit, rub palms against
rough bark ushering in immediacy, animal felt,
superfluity of thought knocked from its branching

out. i am reminded of having. i remind body to embody the thickly snit narrowly scoured blasphemous bliss. consider this warning put on notice what has previously escaped. it is all only finger food.

7

wanting something more. wanting something more is less than what is haved as two. wanting having. having had wants more. having had rarely satisfies. taste dissipates, bowels evacuate emptying to void check it out, void make it out, void wanting want. like your lips like your sips, like your liking liking me. i despise being in need, being having been. i despise being needing when having need rarely satisfies. to put it another way, to place it in a separate drawer, to separate the drawn from the written, the past tense present in ease of being. be all you can having been. rearing all passing tensely into easily in the left lane bowled down. bow before the magistrate, roaring your better side rowing in the splash. lash out as by necessity without frump without pulling in the butt ox pulling cart it away. many roads later many paths now. many roads later many paths now. tiptoe. skip. lay flat grounded in cool clover a cool lover a soon to be. rock on, amigo. rock on.

when too long having been needs by necessity and hasn't had, the i which may have been ceases and fades into someone's nostalgia. like in a photograph, like in a journal of one's undoing done in ink smeared into blurry lines dropped into thoughts evaporated. having been ceases. having been once or twice, remembering liking like yesterday's folded pajamas, like a hot fudge saturday, like elbowing me where it likes to like wanting by necessity by biology by hormonally the twain shall meet. but i missed the twain, heard it choo-choo away, or i dismissed the meet needing taking me elsewhere. so heart to figure, like, go, dude and duddettes with your raisins in the sun with your noses in air conditioned orifices. catch my drifting away. catch my cold outside. catch my thrust up imperious salutation.

can't always be a smile. can't always be having had when wanting needs less difference, less indifference, wanting needs stark yes unblanketed and unflanneled. can you cover me when i'm left out. can you cover me when breezing in. can the clover left outside brought in be here be now be here now without ouch pinch squeeze. without ouch pinch squeeze. without ouch pinch teasing the here and now. or maybe, maybe capitalize OUCH to repeat as often as OUCH, to mince meet often, to often upon occasion when not occupied with done. some despise livers, except when dying, except when their own salvation depends, when needs reduced to minimum, when everything is exactly not needed by necessity. that's where i need to get. that's where gotten halves into whole. in the tomorrow of today, in the twilight of brilliance, the sleep of waking, my eyes knowing only open.

cavernous longings and planetary breath orbit
beneath skin without clue to outer limits of inner
reach, pummeling and pounding, expanse and
contract, a drum's head, my lungs and belly, losing
self to contours, waves, and eddies come lately and
sometimes not at all. how uncivilized that we push
beyond the lips and speak with no speed in swift
archaic tongues and flailing arms and tempering
with the promise of pay. give up get off your belly
ache socked me in the headed nowhere. give up get
off your belly ache socked me in the headed no-
where. repetition bears sublime. fall leaves fall and
leave me alone with gritted teeth dentured, arms
clasped around the pit of desire, flesh ripped,
seasonal flake. how else can express sometimes
shunned, or emote, sometimes shunned, or all the
women and mention primal hold spear to drip
volcanic spew and sit in tall grass ease, body as
nature uncaged, non-subwayed but tracking way
high and way wide as rivers to mountains and shine
burning all.

what we all want is state instating reminding refer-
ral to the grandeur we once were sitting on grand-
pama's knee, bouncing into hope. before. that was
for being before forbearance growled. the gun's
barrel points at us daily so dormantly we shrug off
caving in. blasted. blasted. an explosion not
shunned but of one's doing the many done baked
risen and set on the sill of seriously now and really

now and you've got to be kids know best or do they.

i relinquish respons-a-babblity, this a swath of express, an unwatched gesture not yet disguised or enrolled in a school of thought. pre-elemental and as found as lost as you can get me that napkin, will you.

in breath deep belly shine. run out the door. then in breath deep belly shine. nature evolved me an explorer of cave, mountain, shores of delight and anguishing in longing for food not eaten nor harvested. the least you can do at most arms around the sun setting in my chest rising with mourning the lost and found my keys. nothing musical here unless you can taste it. nothing magical here unless glimpse glee beyond leap cliff harvest moon berated by none. existence knows no stronger taproot. no apologies to those who wish elsewise elsewhere whenever. relish and ketchup everything in small and large portions.

accept completely where are you. resemble yourself as best as possible and disassemble for storage in the box. do both at the same temperature rising and fall asleep to awake from day's dream. snore for others' tasting or sit bolt up wrong in right side up. the best escape plans are often unplanned. be always on watch me headstand, cartwheel, rawspoke in the silence of being. like the light beside bed instead of dark beneath choice. follow me when not leading. i accept your hand in mine, welcome residual flashes,

14

no longer in want of need of separate bed room for the many.

9

listen. i breathe. i breathe you. your leaves against my branches in so many directions listen. listen to yourself breathe me. green passages turn pages stemming out. i listen to hear the lithe and inflatable darkness at the end of beginning to hear.

in echoes mellifluous, many a water's ripple, a sound's wave into being. this darkened chamber of light. this cave without roof. end as a sign to pause before going on. there's no stopping me from red. this ego reflects yours genuflecting and kicking up dirt in my eye that listens. haplessly i breathe listen, fate forfeiting another inspiration. lucky, i suppose.

i lie in search of truth. false appears in every face yet without such disservice, service is not preserved. take a number, wait, turn, stand, sit but not on that sprout. take a stand, sit but not on that puffed proud chest of drawers. what more can i saylisten. what more can i hearfeel. synaesthesia carries passports of all nations and irredeemable looksees. what more can belie this unveiling. hands pull and i am tugged to put out flames to incite others. an apoplectic self. how iridescent of me. this gruff cough unsoffocating excuses with a hand cover. shall we blanket what is preferred unseen. i see

why not, neither here nor there, high nor low, afar
and afraid, sitting on a hill top, gorged on peaches,
gorgeous beyond belief, tender fuzz and slick
juiced. neither there nor here then allwhere any-
way. this jacket unbuttons for breath. this sweater
lifts off this bra. corset of preconceptual thought
unlaces for lashing into the silent noise of dwelling
bodywise. i prefer no other sound movement as
most graceful allegiance to woods, ferns unfolding,
green stems from brown, brown from raven de-
cayed, decay from florid lives in abundance.

race against breath against time in time out while
darkness lights an unclear passage, tooth decaying,
skin flaking. sometimes when i reach out my hand
arms me with touch. sometimes when i hand out
my reach my touch disarms. i know no other way in
to outside, listening to hear, sounding stones,
dancing petals succulent and dry, gasping when
necessary, emboldening the faintly dark spare
stretch of lightfeel.

10

that intimate part of us. when intimates depart from
us. when part of us intimates another. when land-
scapes dream us and we dream of escape as found.
when contours of reason roll like the gentlest of
hills. when we hold ourselves apart from nothing.
when letting go of everything to the stream lands us
the dream. when time as time in no time. when
when how is never and always. soft grass against

skin, summer laze, lax breeze, smooth rocks. as natural as nature beyond the highway, parking lot, microwave, and shoes. dwelling as spleen, elbow, neither my bother nor yours, simply as is

a canyon of simplicity, a cliff of reach, fingers stretched and wedged into crevices of unplanned achievement, image beyond conception. touched with tips of hands, the edge of yours.

11

a self looks for me but darts away. chair offers support but my weight is under pressure elsewhere. path offers direction yet signals cross. mirror reflects absences, tardiness, late slip showing. as if a single point on the horizon. as if a single's bar of couples joining hands. as if determination hesitated, stalled, bus stop that criminal who stole my teeth. bite into that one, will you. even in steadiness, uneven in headiness, body supine, limbs lithe, lilting, asking for touch, clasp, ready as we go around, pebbles rolling off the cliff into the gorge. never

can the same be. a death with every birth right or left behind in the kiln on the copier the front door to return to who left it.

image hides behind sound tra-la, ducks with quacks, lucky, in fact, to stumble into another frequency, new resonance, strings and pluck, a restoration of rhythm shifting keys chords doors and presence as gift of self evading rumors and tumescent lore. ta-da. when not looking refuses to be seen, best to look another way, nod head in delight, spend thrift with speed of light and candle stored as another day not yet understood. anyone else's advice is anyone's else's story, entertaining perhaps, enthralling maybe, a reflection or scintillated distortion or myopic hope brought on by a distillation of disappointment. wait to go on with breathing in plain as fancy as a theurgic urge or merely settling in for a long unsplintered night.

12

what happens in happening hap when doubt dubiously delivers detrimental detritus. what stinging nettle slings a kit or caboodle that tingles snitterly. avoid the ovoid ovulation or adulation stipulated for decided rights-of-way blue-printed, proofed imperfect, a perfunctory magistrated flop of flipping out. singly sentenced as happening haps in doubtful delivery or as an impervious impregnable perception, imagining the unreflected, high-volumed silence. too many questions are questionable, too many answers conclusive, too many conclusions clause-phobic, like a run from the opening, like a spin for your life. i squirm in the constriction, angling and curving to away and get this otter here, get this gee-raffing me.

yet if the detritus is deferred, then it's log jam,

pencil broke, juice cut off, muse dispatched else-
where. an unbearable hat, an indistinguishable fact,
a slap across face it, a tightening below the felt what
like is, isn't, snit or grimace, smile or smoke waft-
ing across the valley of clarity.

13

along with a certain undefined anger, roped in
emotion tied along, wasted, as it were, on happier
occasions, occasionally. stumped by certainly anger,
indefinitely, lasting longer than chords twine and
connect object to object subjectively, like when one
likes wine and another prefers grape juice, sans
alcohol, like when one whines about grapes and
another sips milk happily spilled and shirt soaked.
certainly cause for anger or caused by anger or
angry cravings or misgivings, or merely simply
however a mistake, if, in fact, mistakes are acciden-
tal or, rather, causual via unconscious, my hand
slipping into yours, my words slipping between
yours, your sperm slipping into the forward swim.
not always cause for celebration but causal most
certainly.

rising like a swell, despised for smelling, nosing into
another's business, supposing a desperation, a hasty
glance in a westerly direction, winds originating
northerly, spins originating motherly, wearing a
snug paternity suit, swearing at the creases and
seems like something doesn't fit as presupposed,
expectation lit up like a birthday cake yet doused

before the blowing of the wish. justified anger. anger in the knick of time. time kicked in the shin by, surprise, not what we expected, but a bitterest cake, crummy as all get out, go on, give in, give up. give in, give up. give in yet somehow going on, given circumstances not expected. not so swell after all. after all is said and done it again. gave, gave, gave it all away, but now, now, now getting it back through anger. just. not what's expected but the same differently as emotions rolls and foils our best efforts, our fronting and backing out of commitment.

14

what i'm trying to say cannot be said it too many times in other words shadowing facets unknowingly streamlined and disguised in feathers and sequins. what i'm trying is happening not and yes but reaching out simultaneously reaches in as doors swing both directions. but doubt. but doubling. but dubbing mine for another's look sound more compatible, compatriotic, complicitous. comes and do's that don't negate the equatorial balance or orbital ease but rotate and rotate and unseemly so sequential as inhale to ex, as blood to flow, as fem as none.

leaps bound up. cries out down. run in soft petalled soles because my place meant for someone else, my place yielded to the louder, the larger, the expectant one anticipating rightful place and we the wronged, we the misrepresented, weeds absorbed in fanciful misdeeds and hobbies, pulled up or out and loaded down, silenced, clammed in calm, dubbed no doubt, fretting in forgotten egregiousness, composted to recompose another's lot not our own, not our own it and claim in doubled tongue, lick lick perfection.

15

tomatoes and rubies. red eye socket. ricocheting superlatives. this is beginning the only way i know how to undo what is unknowing to scrape surfaces to dip and dive so very humbly in the soil of ancestors, the toil of feet and hands, the skinning of hopes and fearing authoritarian rules booting me, slapping gloves and worsening conditions, cold kitchens, cold hearts, older ways enforced while bent ever closer to the floor, trammeled, trampled. at the level of mice, fallen rice, spirits withdrawn from displays of affection, affectation, cultural pride deteriorates to disdain one's racing to get ahead, planting dreams, breath sifting soil like worms crawling and cultivating.

liberty thrives in privacy, hides in crawl spacing out, appearing bored, with drawing land escapes, natural word with no humans present, none tense, no perfunctory attempts at cutting trees, seeing wood, carrying water, igniting flames for warmth, degrees of pleasure, inspirited, uninhibited, at home in home on the ranging of imagination, sensual reality awakening skin and bone, the moment of diurnal

kinship with leaf, book, and road, decision a veined
and multi-volumed path.

16

i am empty handed and mindless, pockets thread-
bare from items unsold. projections know no fools.
all's wise in the queendom of come ons and shrug
offs.

within the realm of possibilities, could be a hand-
shake, could be firm and floppy. could be a milk
shake stirred, prelude to disaster, plaster from walls
falling to bits on manuscripts and look the other
way. could be sitting in your office, my words as
yours, your words as mind your own business,
probe into spectral difficulties which hide behind
bushes and barks and shouts suppressed with a leash.
unleash you say, while others say mummy, what's
that. let the earth go. let the flesh slip from gripping
so tightly to understanding like a flash of thought for
the day dreaming ease mind that craves understand-
ing. slip cool body into cool pool to limber limbs to
float and dive, wet hair, wet skin, whet appetite for
sensual delight outa mind. we live too much in the
frame. we slip to oft from the flame, feet planted,
staked to our stake, remembering witches burn and
shying away, slying from the seer whose knowing
brings on her crisp demise. creepy in a pedophiliac
sort of way. creepy the way spirit constantly de-
ceives and loosens sleeves and lost sleep in a dream,
a whisper at night with a few trusted friends. the

informing breeze that soothes and lifts hairs, the informal sneeze that leaves the host discomfited or running out of room of one's own, as is necessary, put on order, then on hold

down the fort, hold your horses, holding the bolt in place while enemies bust the door down. such turvy topping, such laughable breaches, such pitiable minutiae, so many piles of dirt across the floor sweeping the horizon.

open then shut for clear space empty of disturbed word, empty of worn textiles, souvenirs of pasts vacated and a present wrapped, paper bagged, or ephemerally veiled. this compulsion like a sapling urging tree, branching my tendencies, twigging thoughts, unfurling leaving behind fall and winter to spring an irresistible moon, a glow of momentary knowing, path of light, flow, and stepping lightly upon leaves and go fully embodied.

17

from my lips escape breath, silence speaking truth. only my toes know, not even my hairdresser. only unfolding my clothes in orange hues. only the orangutans running from flaming brush into traps of poachers. only the birds fleeing while trees topple from saws. deeply in the moment. pliant hands. wings delight by fleeing death, my silence escapes. the breath, the ease, the flesh deepening, limbs stretching beyond known states into foreign countries. visitors welcomed, regardless of tongue lashing or silence. barbed wire cuts into too many memories. loaded guns aim at innocence, dam streams, screams, and bubbles of laughter. serious when threats exists, serious when belts sear flesh, when song vanishes, when dance stills. i court impermanence, beguiling teacher, remembering to forget, forgetting to remember, bracing to embrace what eludes grasp, holding nothing, your hand, my wanting you inside, me sliding into relief root breath. only this silent kiss.

18

to write one cannot think. to sleep one cannot drink. to write one two three blend sounds me out off centered marginally by millimeters measured without spoonful of sugar the medicine drowns me. this sweet imagining. this neat chaos of blur frowns and scoffs and wading between reefs and thighs, churn of circadian rhythms. bowing before the crown of this process. stop. open to the flow of this recess receding and advance, commence, and tweet, tweet, tweet. stop.

go. go on. go off hesitantly. hands in pockets, skirting hiking up.

no one here but homegrown. no one spared but moan as loud as can, as proud as man pounding chest, as planet circling ego or however you go, have gone before, have placed it on the mantle,

have carried it off the mantle, have carried it off
with such finesse that no one questions and many
imitate, hoping for a similar scope, sloping down
their own valley to view the tiny people, the spine-
less people, those pining for brighter skies, fuller
bellies, larger cars. park your habits at the door.
hold your rabbits by the ears. mark your calendars
with off color remarks. white out later. fight it out
later. find out later the extended damage extending
your life shortening your breath shortening your
hair a cut above the shoulder, a cut above the rest it
on the mantle or carry it to the rest home, the best
home, the hone in on the prairie and canary my
thought, be wary of the onslaught of images sublime
from medieval times, from somewhere between
evil and goodness gracious. thanks and welcome and
arrivederci and pontiac and rutabaga. whassa matta.
got corn between your toes, string between your
teeth, strung out between a rock and a heart place,
a hearth flaming wildly and one long cooled, so
cool, dude, like a frozen pot pie, like a husband and
a why not, a tied knot, a sly drifter, a cry from the
passage of time, a knock upon awareness's door
which floors you. open

windows to draft a new message, to craft in the
gentle waves or turbulent engine revving, striving,
combusting. a compost of the mind is thought from
every where, all hairs, pointing fingers, easy strides
and less extreme fractures of significant ribbing me
where it counts, tickling skin, shimmy and shine,
shimmy and shine. this, a matter of posture. this, a
matter of putting to pasture thoughts dead-ended,

25

hairs split, borrowings shelved into forgotten origins, wheat never harvested, crops rotted, cops spotting erroneous displays of disingenuity, an engine stalled, tires flattened or rubbish, rubbish, rubbish piled high carpet, an eye sore, an earth sore, eventually a musical score for off-off broadway, those thinking they're on to something, put off by typical turn on, those left in the right of center stage, those staging their fears, those careening careers, tired, excited, or open windowed, cooled by the craft.

19

she feels urgencies, blocked breath wanting passage. trying not to control, she controls in her trying. she lets go. lets urgencies of the written right her in step with heart. she steps out of the written, loses herself, having already lost. freedom in anonymity and synonymy. lit figures stand in doorways. careful creases a skirt that please symmetry. silence and sound vie for attention. lips part. clouds part. only breath. only desire. only

trickle, splash, tiered rice fields where she dwells.

a man's voice calls. a woman's voice. man's she listens, compelled by low pitch, belly resonance, softening, a reminder of animal footing, scent. breath. seething. quietly upset siphoning criticisms carried on wind to be lifted, carried, scent unseen. torn. transcendent. luminous. she wants burn, but pauses in vocation instead.

breath wings, breast wings, templates for soul, contemporaries who rarely doubt deeds but instead rant hoorahs and atta girl. the patch that was bald, the patch that was barren, the patch caught as sneeze, as bent knees, as needing so much of don't have, of absences in presence of rarified virtues underappreciated, under bed clothes, under pleated skirts and pleasures not mine but waiting in the want, not wanting to wait through forms signed, signed off, formless. so discouraging to sidestep worlds, whirls, the be's, the have-nots impoverishing multifold whirls straightened by reason slow motion and lights.

20

reservations slip past into the moment's urgency. slippery breaks give reason cause to pause. a castration complex, a situation complexity, a knick in the speed of time for naught, naughtiness, and nothing left for haughty pride. the barricade breaks open the moment's surgery, a cut from necessity, a split apart, a grievance applying to earth core persistencies. my feet have lost their foot hold me up. my streets have paved the story in another well-plotted directionless. greet me, i say not. give to me, i say not either now nor then nor on your front stoop back up. it's all because of nothing. it's all because i

forgot my lunch meet me at the corner, will you. i
will myself willingly at destiny's door stooping over
the mess it up grievously. i yield to all causalities,
ripped flesh, wounds that wouldn't and shouldn't
that haven't, not yet anyway, but i'm waiting any-
way somehow for yes always awesome. a crep...a
creep, an intruder alert, a wake up and smell the
coffin before you lie in your rot.

the critic's miserly attempts pull the rug out from
below the desk at dusk, the miserable defunctive
ineffective lead weighted seat abased by quivering
lip service stationed over see it, there goes a gain
into loss. how many times must the tutor's wander-
ing eyes, feet tapping, hand tipping milk, illness of
deficit, apathy apparent in the masses racing on low
highways in their lowdown upstart sideways
screwed on tight lost it glares. reactionary, i'd say
not. devolutionary, i'd not say either weather suits
me fine. a corruption of heart baked singled out
fortuitously coupled in an intermix interbake
racially challenged stereotype of flaunting. try not
to stand on the same stoop over. try not to single
me out as separate from the restfully asleep, deep in
dream, waving palms overhead, a heard. what we
ignore

kneed with attention, clap hands, dust off offensive
powders that take away from claiming the right
from being and been. i can only authenticate with
sonic feeling, harmony amid dissension. where is
fee...where is feeling...where is fitting into the
insurrection or the resurrection or the lift of spirits

imbibed in a plastic glass too fast too slow or never tasting the liquid from the flask, never bamboozling, never coming clean or claiming rightful ownership to impropriety, sobriety, propped up by invalidity, invalidness, lividly living the lie. lions, tigers, and bears.

21

why is it that i refuse to believe or refusals push outside the guardian's door, beyond the banyan tree, outside the carry on anyway. why is it that mere belief minus feeling mirrors absence mirrors empty hands mirrors a minus not plush velour comfort, arms in embrace, symphony of heart, accord like an accordion player at our table. why that i refuse to reuse yesterday thought about it. why so used to refusing the blow out sparked a separation from the family from the heart from the self home. how to lick relish lick pickle lick salt. how to pick a pepper, peek a sneak, and run spin in place. how to i know. how to know i speak hush your silent frictions. how to. how to. how to free. how to lead the follow. how to follow the literate literally. how to here it is, here it spins frenetically.

22

continually pulled to watery scapes away from form, hard edges egging me complete form, to harden, edge my way into matter, no slight pit-

tance, no height too high, no climb too cumber-
some. a dense shrubbed mountain sideways glance.
a thicket of blowing breezeways, sneeze, and luxury
interior. ask questions, they said, not but do. what
questions, i said yet do not listen do not speak do
not sit down beside the watery escaping land scavat-
ing body craving body cracking, fissures, so many
muddy fissures, soft and reach the edge, stretch
hands, palms out, fingering along ledges, along
guesses that raise questions, eyebrows, lo-brows
and hi there.

from hardness into flame darting core rising, blink,
pine trees yielding to cones, pining beckoning a
larger bush, seed a smaller hush up. my silence goes
eastward. my obeyance closes eyes, darts open and
flares public displays of lacerations, gruff snickers,
sickening applause as conform to rules, silence inner
sway, musical spheres interfered with until heat
rises, irises expand, looking as linking without dried
eyes, without frenzy, with nasal misgivings,
hunches, and cloves.

it is you touching in the delicacy of urgent. how
much clearer in my misgivings, how much mistaken
in my coping, how much gathering at the stems,
wilting, blooming, eyes blossoming with rage,
fecund as blaze.

23

this threshold articulates a muddy passage.

24

i struggles at this emergence. i slumbers at the
threshold bottom stare, bottom step away from the
ladder lest bad luck falls over springs here. i grap-
ples, gropes, pokes fun, slaps cheeks, chides the
chosen, craves the unavailable, pushes away, staying
awake past bedtime for school. streak mean. broken
chains. humid earth. toil. toil till sweat soaks cloth,
till soil coats wet every arid tongue, every livid lie.
i flares at incertitude and shy suns and twilights. i
craves leaping over thresholds, ignoring dogs'
growls, festering guards who let down their rancor,
who hesitate, who blink at thoughtless thinking
again, speaking so plainly, leading the blind into
sighing, the broken to repair, those forced into exile
to return temple bound. i jokes at the haughty smug
in forgetfulness.

i places herself in himself for mingling a flutter to
vibrate into articulation. hear me in this silence.
listen to the vague. expound on false truths truth-
fully with a grin and barely seated but stepped over
threshold, feet on either side, indentured yet free,
clasped hands, and bare-footed, eyes looking into
the impenetrable silent scramble in spirited quest,
knowing only feel, only letting go in the balance of
water and fire, palm on this vertiginous earth.

25

who is spoken.

26

between lush felt sonic inharmonia trend crevices pleading with velvet sweeps, templates of solace, of sentiments, of craving satisfied, of no desires, no designs upon nature, nothing either native or noteworthy or indicative of someplace else. here in lush amplitude, in abundant embrace smile guffaws hilarity, in so many hands giving receipt, so many fingers tipping scales, so many tips hidden inside fortune cookies, so many cooks stirring soup, such scents in so many sentences without words. my refusal enters sorrowfully into bliss. my disdain rides high proudly in yielding a seat. i sit down, bow down, look and leap, listen but don't speak up, don't hook up the filter, don't bend down and out. yes to do. yes to amplify. yes to loosen the lock down, the break down, the heck yes. belly vibrates as bellies bravely expound into obese exclamations. a right on fuck off potato blight.

order in the court. order in the count your chickens, your change of heart attack, switch hit. record in the court. record how chickens flee as slight motion, the flapping of wings, the clapping of stick it in the fiery place furiously. watch fur and feathers burn. in lush abundance all comes fortuitously. letting go is not knowing, releasing the plow, tumbling down hill, upping the ants, whatever antics fit or don't you listen to me. this muscular squeeze wants release. this mustard seed wants planting. this you must see. come here, will you not, will you always speak so poorly, will you always peak when you're not supposed, not in position, full of opposing views, those who flew above the barn and up the hill. i cast my glance away. i give up my bill folding clothes. look and rocking chair, my step scratches ground while stellar is my reach, my i belonging elsewhere, roams into yours elsewhere beside the point. how dull

floods of sensation. surround me with drum vibrates awakening my fossilized listen, unraveling my mummified touchiness. always comes back to history. always returns like a homing pigeon, home for the holidays, wanting returns oceanic waves the entire spectrum while simultuously a singular thread, a singular hue cast as me or an utterance to deepen breath and flood the field with watery eyes and watery beginnings in amphibious crawling in and out. shed skin to widen wings to articulate gesture in crisp sounds perfectly amplified in starry skied amphitheater.

27

a simple thread weaves entirety. the ego dangles without believing. they lived happily after thought. they survived merrily without thinking. they

usurped their erroneous ways, gave them away to
the salvation army.

28

i chance this. wave goodbye, erase myself, delete
codes of misbehavior and antics up my sleeves and
seeing you in as kindly step aside and follow me into
the darkness to glow wormy and lighter, please, and
speak up to no good waving to extremes of pleasure
and painful creases in the belly devoid of feeling
your arm around my shoulder my burden, shudder-
ing with your my your my your confusion of identi-
cally twined tendencies to let go of absurd remarks
that don't do don't deliver the pizza and don't do
don't deliver the good evening good morning and
better after we finish eating and earn more dollars
through beg your pardon, if you don't speak upward
mobility, then we'll have to cap your handicap your
cacophonous ways way way beyond the ocean, see
breeze, release the lock, break the locket, sun glare
in eyes, close lids, spreading wings to otherworldly
adventures without passport, without packing
necessities like ties and address kindly no one but
those who address you in kind with your own needs
in mind in hand in ballyhoo, don't try to brave the
gusts by selfishly holding onto stamp the ground,
smash what intricacies no longer serve, suffice it to
say, your needs, what bleeds the instinctive desire
for no things but food, shelter, humanity rolled into
a vice, placed in oil, jarred in action, always reac-
tion.

where to start is where starting is. starting is at the beginning with ends in sight while blinded by lightning rod and nodding fitfully asleep. a most purposeful mess. a must surreptitiously disguised as frankincense intensely huffed. entering centering. entering through the exit blocked open. centering with the outside shaped inward on the periphery outlined in the margin. centering with entranced by music high-volumed when low in spirits. blow up the spirits, inflatable and indefatigable. faith that. face that. face off the entrance centered on the edge being elsewhere here and there in a syncopated telepathic spree. sip spritzer when need be when be need when knees knock when how are you come in. such suchness of the noxious delight of emitted strands of illogic. throw a pebble. stick a twig. stick a pebble in the thrown away. throw way in three ways or a forte night and *buenos noches* and heed the knock now knock now open please come in.

fitfully and snippy i edge my way centrally locution. reason edges in shrinks and coyly hides behind corners having asserted, having dominated, having won the ball game. pitch again beyond the horizon. speech again beyond the ventriloquy. confessedly knowing no other way but this speckled calamitous snap of awareness wearying, wearing this way-wardly, or however the faint shall fit or nitpick nitpick nitpickity uppity snowballing as the crow flies or the cry flows trying the best way possible impossibly reasoned, posturing or disguising full

awareness of the beginning as a brilliant light so
blinding so binding that i, yes, i yield to the weight
and cannot wait this moment and want the next and
want what's not so because this is so.

30

my apologies. my kneeling down. my best wishes.
my sorriest sentiments. my bowed head. my heavy
heart. my my. my my my. my oh my. my oh why.
my why not. my knotted way. my way of not
saying. my say way for sorrying. my worrisome
apology. my plea for forgive it away. my place for
grave donations. my my for you you. you you you
sublime. you so upright. you so tangle free, cleanly
bright, openly clear. you you likening me my. why
my like you as your. your your my. your acceptance
of my my. your most excellent stance on the
floored me. your me as my we. may we.

31

on a precipice. on the slippy ice. on the inside. on
the mellifluous scents that transport pace and cries
out for no reason enough. caught by understanding,
snared in the trap clap flung open. screech of the
horned owl, reach of the homing in, widened
window door, the edge of mind's understanding,
ungraspable, gaspable. palpitations of health assert-
ing rightful place, feet planted on earth, ears open,
eyes wide, touch asserting felt body, soft and pliant

with resilient core.

what they say shouldn't happen but rarely. what they say is so so what. what they say becomes my say before a subsequent separation oh so divisively. sliced apart to integrate. separated wholesomely. should happen could. could snare but on the slippity precipice won't. might cry out, might fly off, might mighty as owl's screech or more magnificent beast. a blast in delicate firm steps, heated core rising featherward high and rootedly low. oh so sinuous. oh so elegiac centering. i can only smile wryly. i can only open my hide. i can only spread arms and contradict every edict flying my way.

32

my return. my return as only i can. this exposure, this infinite solitude reaching ancestral family. only return, this regular proceeding, path as heart beat, this awareness. only i. only i locked free in form. these eyes, these ears, skin, nose, tongue, only i. yet i yearns and pleas for you. to please you or console or conjure or take me by the hand and run away to here together. come back with me, back to back with me. connected to stellar cells, returned to that ocean pacing me, this my infinite reach, my final part apart from none.

my skin chaps. my eyes blink. my skin sees you walk, laugh, and lean away towards me. all is relationship, regress or digress, dressing for success, whatever that is, whatever all is, whatever is none of it. my reach seeks space. my seek paces my reach, emblazons it in hot lettered neon glory solitude. such glow in this diminutive state, such heat.

this beat knows none other. this beat complies with larger laws. oh blood scheming in polyphonic paths tracking me to you returning in all ways never the same always something different, a pea in the pasture, a needle in the haywire. this my plea and pleasure, this my your beat, the pulse race in time enough without frowns.

33

expansive strokes of color and arms widening in bold display of reactive fluorescence. heavenly sighs wisteria draping across chairs lounging in the labor of creation. why this is so because. the purity of reactive responsibility. toes cutting into sand, a sublime beauty as ugly as all get out come in. to get even wilder, uneven in wilderness, spent in the march to destroy the beauty of begun at the start with no end in sight, no sighs but steady birth, inhale, the extremes in between, pleasantries dropped like an unnecessary frock and fraudulent behavior peeled off and on to something, no, not better, but something peeled off, to put it bluntly, to say so plainly, to say nothing as something in simple fact of the matter, the *primae materia*, primates swinging high and my own desires yielding to

laws little understood, little too big for pea brains
no matter how many bran muffins and cheerios
consumed. to obliterate this self by yielding, no
stop sign, but yielding, giving way without saying
hey, buddy, what's up around the corner, but
waving on, continuing in the way of ancestors, cell
companions staying put, laying low, laughing
quietly and snickering at the doodles and licking the
loose lips preening and rearranging to let go of this
ever present need to pinpoint exactly, to realize
exactitude, to bow before the reign of reason.
instead uproar upright chairs and tableaus and
return to the diaphanous music of the spheres, the
verbal play that delights in splash lusciousness
without need to measure and define and demean
and demote like a choke hold like a choke hold, like
a remove your hands from my neck, remove your
stand from my pastoral leanings for this tendency to
return to cells emerging in the field steam mountain
peek of glory before all was codified and qualified.
let us hold hands and play.

34

tug boated back and forth, tugged and bloated.
there's more between than meets the eye, more
between what's bifurcated, myopically speaking,
languagables limiting expression laughably, argua-
bly, despite writers' best attempts otherwising. how
else though, my synonymous, can this existence be
seen without deflection and revision. how now
brown callous, periodically, semitically, struggling

with the tug of hide and seeking far and widening
horizons beyond the jet stream beyond the secured
channel beyond the known into the dream felt as
the hairs of this arm.

35

when to begin when has begun which is correct and
rightfully placed but when, as if waiting for the bell
chime, as if taunting the chilled lime or some taste
that compels and lingers, triggering pleasure not
aversion, tight hold released, pressure relieved,
pleasure restored neutrally like a bouncing neu-
trino. often waiting for an appropriate cue when
sometimes maybenotalways but sometimes the cue
is ignored, wrongly stored or mistaken as a bullet
dodged, so phone doesn't ring or call calling lacks
absence present for a beginning. sometimes neck
bent against wind and sand, trial a start which trails
a start and provides a hanging onto something.
gratefully we sigh. (notice my shirking of responsi-
bility.)

glam cram rot this morphic passing out away from
the bridge into a greater larger widening path.
always in pursuit of a *juste mot* or the radically
shifted horizon that calms the beast but rouses the
breast from den of dominant refusals of the orders
that obliterate and obstruct the run across the pass,
the sprint up the mountain sliding into a heaven of
our making, a wilderness passing into a public
sphere ranging wildly as imaginatively possible. in

this chaotic rule where form asserts its own benign dominion, my raiments fall away, my clips and constant queries quiet to mere seeing, mere hearing, mere abstemious luxuries. expression blends in distinct solitude, wavering branches and sobriety of felt soles to the earth, hair bristling like a bear's paw against a den of inequity. my your our obsequious pursuits find berries of every stripe and blaze in my mind like a lover's hot kiss and yesterday's near miss. oh fervent musk. oh odious projections pretending to belie knowledge but oh so rotten milk curdled around my finger and bellicose surroundings. we cannot forget what's most important unless we forget to remember the importance of forgetting. this i forget and continually remind meagerly wandering in the roundabout walkabout, the pout and sneeze while the hairs of my arm and the twitch of eye suggests another path be taken, the road less tarred, the toads leaping out of bear's way kissing ground with snout, licking ground without pout. i enter my den, bare earth exposing all.

36

and let go. and pretend as if iffing were not more than less a fragment of spacious environs, a craggy shore rock laden drive way out. this pretentious ramble simplifies life moronically like a seismic wave relieving response time to a mere incalculable few minutes flat rising out of the smoke the ashes the flipped out state we speed away from we very much despise and run wildly fiery footed with

forgotten memories of the beloved one two theatri-
cally stepping off stage while hoping for applause or
recognition beyond the obituaries because never in
our right mind left overs best when warmed upside
down. listen to my niece who grieves for mice.
spice the dish with ragged choices or whatever's
available. beggars can't afford to be chastised, not
that anyone else in their right marbles rolling off the
table onto the floored. further flurrying but not in
haste makes the pituitary gland work over tenu-
ously. other secretions secretly despise such claus-
trophobic calculations which is the way the sum
parts always equal what's leftover, stored in close
quarters beside the bowling bawling over spilled
mice. little sniggerlies lie beside the point. tiger
lilies sprout in fertile solitude as walt witwoman
once said. (why has she not been mentioned; why
this wife of high

esteem shed from books.) why the shekhinah so
many argue against, quit rallies, round surreptitious
armies, wrangle their cronies against the between as
feminist plot of land to be developed and plotted
against. i make no apologies, offer no promulgations
of vitriolic crackers because many oppose the lass
and use crass methods institutionalized as high art
veiled as wisdom. i get off the subject on the object
objecting to offenses to flesh soft and pliant against
the hard arm, the rammed iron of push comes to
shovel this in deep do not come any closer despite
welcoming naturally some irate fragment delivered
with a quick punch in belly smoted hilarity machine
of regress and force. my own approach typically is

less typhoonal unless my ire roused, unless my siren awakened, unless practiced instinct lumbers with deliberate claws to protect this vital glow.

37

here presently as smooth silver sleekly applied. here jeweled in breathtaking majesty upon simplicity's throne of recall, porously clothed, palatially roomed in the wood of exit. always he and she. they hold handlings except when sensations driftwood away from aware of looking inward. dangers lie within unless unsheltered by the storm of foolishness. steps, crevices, bending down on all fours, frowns forgotten like renewable crop harvested, seedlings break surface dust to gleam of presence. the mist of a pertinent smile grin and mysteriously appearing in the vanishing moment of gales and slighter breezes. a return to breath of terrestrial core of fabric ligamented to skin path to quiescent as a calm pool of thought stirred by a frog's leap or the dip of a willow's branching awareness. inner tree delights, roots and barking dogs who chase cats for fun. fun. funny as a fumble in dark price crisp cool humble drop, this a weather system passing through. my request is an orbital one, to revolve the doors and redress wounds and lichen moss to reforest an arid temperament, as balance as heart of wind swept valley.

my touch sways delicately winged in the feather of
this moment. again now. again. bereft yet full of pot
holes and dreams refusing to sleep in the bed tucked
too tightly, the dream rising like smoke like a
handshake like a yearning for global ease. sigh.
velvet glistening sun set in the morning while
grieving for birth. contradictions marry to live
happily as after thought before an over bleached
pragmatics. my request beside rice and soy to lie
beside my synonymous aware of steady breath
watchful as an infant's sleep deep in the center,
swept in the current steadily drifting lull and toss of
the present.

you hold out your handle with care. you kindle your
hair as an inflammatory remark. you mark score
delete delight so that i as you when we brave ele-
ments, pulling the hood closer around our necks,
hauling the push what's nasty away, look the other
away from the stinging nettle, the meddling into
another's business, and lie down with me on this
soft down bedlam, loom your hand around my your
bent over, sleep, dream, creep ever so slowly into
the mist we step, listen, glee as gloating, flee as
arriving in this moment fur lined coat of habits
tossed to the stinging wind. we take this moment to
thank think thought about it before but now's timid
rule of passing away before it leaves forever, before

it steals swiftly into that good night, sleep well, see you in the moon light. thanks as i hold onto the letting go. thanks as you hand over, as you ham it up, as you vegetate your animation. i am in knowing, that state of minding my own busy laziness, my own given away in an estate sale without tags and plunders. i, too, soften under your carrying me away on your shoulder, your arm, your branch cuttings warm as hearth. this i must acknowledge, this faithing of ledges near the falling off, the spindly drift, creeping ever so quietly in a solitude of yearned bliss. my forgetfulness will likely surface after an underwater extreme, but such is the coarse coat, the hoarse throat, my tendency to delinquent mastery into the corner, though now it's fine to join the group, to plead causes and not plead because lacking is haved and desire's flame warms with a hot chocolate.

40

and yet the deep furrow of feet deep in grounded earth with sky hat and arms luxuriant in breeze and breath opened as a blossom and wheeze and sniff insinuating nothing but every single celled creature allowed their slow or swift developmentally challenged succeeding in succession in a frequency that more than a few hear, this i say not in so many words, singular utterances, singed eyebrows, songs never vocalized or recorded for any tape loop-de-loo. i for one as two and more prefer to preview a rain check and what the hell bent heaven scent of this fortuitous collapse clapping and lip synching with a muffled roar. have i failed to mention my pleasure. have i mailed my unmentionable pardon, ambiguous twist of paraphrase, parachute opening on time as if time delineated when feet hit the ground or merely scrape grass or preferably land with a cloud's ease. such pleasantries escape notice when gravity's law space out. sometimes out of mind is better than not home at all or detoxed or that wily fox is at it again. she returns again and again. she brings him along for the rise. he sifts through the collection of cells, watering and wasting away, sleeping, rising on her commands never articulated.

accuse me not of your divisiveness. take responsibility for a walk around the block headed. my own motion insinuates you and you applaud closure and beginnings, jars opened, flowers watered, decay approached like any dust. i am not bleeding in this landing, my feet touching grace, your garden widening like a smile.

41

slowly. blissfully. weathered. mended fractures. cloudless scheme. rinsed pastel in *crème de menthe*. all's in order in gated waywardness. fingers bend like spine. hands reach like stem. rays of light blend unveiling wisps and extremes of form, sculptural and sepulchral. the domed temple of galaxy, incense wafting on wings, opens doors, penned in this book.

disappearances vanish. the mad go crazy. delirium gives way to wishes wantonly planted in rows and circles crop up, spiral into a child's imagination and an artist's muse. less extreme is more. more seams unravel, dreams boil, more lessons of heartfelt joy. slowly in breath's colored labyrinth, full palette of possibilities for brush stroke, breath stroke, lithe lilies, silly games, flame embraced in the summer's winter.

42

and yet again finding the flaw relapse the crisply ironed denial steering passions away in crinoline skirts and requiring issues of import take front seat or get side swiped, swept away in sweat, though neatly, though ordered, though cataloged. by necessity of sanity and replacement of worn batteries and banter with a bugle warning troops of the coup smashes reason and grins and spins yellow. my plasma boils. my raspy throat attempts any wire, any scene, many figures of speechlessness amplified a thousand times over and between you and me in the intimacy of this cloth and the cloven hoof. flaw, of course, is judgment adjudicating the administering of catalog from flyers, brandy from the wine of your idiosyncrasies. let petals unfurl as they may or in april. let each strand of striated matter decline growth or dismiss missives of destruction. rocks slide from cliffs no matter the mesh reinforcements, concrete pronouncements, the signs suggesting one route better than butter or a marginal existence. the

realization, if you will, if willing, if willful, is in the
revelation, coat removed, skirt and pants fallen to
heights of despairing joy and ascent of whimsy. why
degrade such feminine expressions whose jaws well
spared and softened by years of rolling in mud
splashing in the river of laxity. get beneath the
covers of scold. the scent bent on prodigious warn-
ings and alarm filling to the lifest, for vesting the
storm quell desire unavoidably. why surmount
anything less surpassable or extreme. diminish in
nothing. speculate only when the immeasurable
laughs face forward with hind sight. blast in the
reverie of revelry, balloon and streamers, debates
and stories not withstanding or slumping in the
cornered rise of the fall. realize everything as
nothing more or less. rest in the restlessness of
elbows knocking doors ajar and doors jarring to
extreme. extreme expletives by example exit
excess waste, excessive morsels, successive replen-
ishments necessary by nature's neo-cortal rump,
pardon my french fries, pardon my egregious refusal
to tone down, to bake cookies, to apron such
tendencies. imperviousness knows no gender
boundaries and only consults aestheticians when
coughing ceases to cease and muscles please not
even the gruff guard, the geek meekly but wisely
and weekly but kindly offering the seat to none,
regardless of apathy, sympathy and fat bill folded.

this my step wet hygiene. this your majestic balus-
trade illustrating a material witness of such import
that all bow in gratitude or collapse in laughter on
the floor. such saturnalia. such mercurial wayward-

ness. such an obvious igloo of shortcomings that despite palm leaves and jaws wired shut, in-laws, by-laws, and entrance exams, exit by the lit signs only, flavor the popcorn and toss the uncooked kernels.

43

she who is nowhere going any place fast gets up and down, takes anti-depressants, fakes laughter, drinks water, and streams for musing for leaning on friends for fortitude, for their stream-line cars, their other-ness, their vivacity she claims lacks in herself, clacks in herself, noise beyond annoyance beyond lowered volume beyond madonnas and whores and other women of grand repute. she who is nowhere going anyplace fast drinks gleefully the emptiness, thirsty for rest these weary bones, test this fractured heart, unless a ticket locks her in place out of place, not in solace, without necklaces, neither those with briny trinkets nor those with glistening jewels which strangle anyway, which tangle in her get out of here as fast as can, as crass as a drunkard stumbling off the curbing his desires not. this is the way she rots in place, nods to her tots in spaces heated, in visions she refuses to pursue because they turn her reason black and blue, forgetting as she often does a wider imagination, a cider warmed up late at night makes quite a decent drink. always drink. always drink with the rank and order life in untangled web, a more manageable thread that rolls away, off the curb, down the gutter into the clutter of the cut it out, all this space meant for someone else's parked butt, someone else barks up that tirade. this way in space meant elsewhere rushing to pass forth to move directionally accused of turning too far to the left of right on, m'lady, said a passerby with no drink in hand but left this off-hand, off-color remarkably. she thanked him nonethesame differently from before this mess of racing nowhere quickly, pacing herself with erasures of centuries and expectations of motherhood and neighborhood and tupper wears her out. she takes the pill for depression, her iron long broken, long past mending creases, wrinkling where might have been a twinkle, a canvass, an ambition beyond what her fathermother, sisterbrother, enemyfriend, all wise counselors she listened to once upon a time before all was unhappily after. she pressed her lips forth, she sealed her pips closed, she wheeled her cartwheels, her smart deals, her demonic laughter, and inhaled a pillage of senses, devoured a course on intracoastal waterways and when she could, when she could, she c-c-came as long as possible racing nowhere swiftly as you can say supercalifornia. this is not a sad stormy nor a mad groom ranting at his brigadoom who once looked so delightful in her veiled coyness, her unrealized self smarting inside corset and bravo. i can not tell

i can not yell

this word

watch my lips, this told by she

who figured out none of the above correctly an-
swers the unasked questions displace modifier
humidifying dry flaky skin. all is nothing less than
more liquefaction of stupidity and lucidity.

44

she he mean me you her well best. he we forever
next seeming. whenever i you together alone sit
down. i you like want need forget it. remember to
pleasure pain sit sneeze okay. forgot the reminder
for him we they said it again never. in plain ba-
roque. in a stained shirt sleeve in a painted patina.
they we our saw blindly the smirk and marked
down. they we recall forgetting. we you synony-
mous embrace. my diet gorges on you them then
next. my his sight slighted near or forestry, tapestry
of amaze meant for viewing. when now later. feel
me you. caress the strike of a pose pleasurably
inciting heat, burn, desperation quieted as dripping
sap. speak holler listen to no one me. listen to this
hold released as panther lick and owl hoot. press
ever so delightfully lunging straight to the twist of
the narrow expanse. remember what hesitation
betrayed. remember the tray spilled upright and us
they licking the sponge. never. just like we did
when we didn't. just like didn't does on sundays and
windy afternoons when rain pelts the tent canvas
and trees drip with dew. i them offer breath cur-
rently passing, currently squelched opening like a
daisy, such floral devastating breach of trust. but

honestly he her lies together united in limbs and branches pruned and ripe fruits for pluck and verve. squeeze her him yet. i offer what they have. they give away what i don't. we belief nothing always in deep prayer pleading for remembering the salient touch, the heat cooled, the cry burning flesh to arise. we sit, yes, while standing for our inner life, that vacuous abundance, this clearly vague, that this for those less often, frequently forbidden or simply lost on the way.

way out in. all the way stopped. a lush velvet stripped bare to stripes and polka dances. such loud quietude, humble brazenry, and spiced noodles. we you delight in the feast, their appetites appeased ceaselessly. when now later. i want you them we. i want sleep dream wake up. they leave alone with them. we can't stand to sit still. we're still moving nowhere. they seem to know everything

about nothing that matters. your formula is rash. his her rash is itchy, makes me you dissolve in tears. floor us with your sky. adore us with scornful admonishments of nothing. bleed the silence of this azure sky. save us to let go this captivity for details that mean, mean, mean little more than less meas- urable. you touch me deeply on the surface and i'll not have you do it again and again and again when today not then yes by extremes not by the tree inside this outrageousness. pick sting peel. stick your heel in your mine. these thoughts are few and far. those links connect my intimacies to delicate wings that fly far nearly missing you. can we. have we. do don't they. yes, let's go. yes let go.

45

as if this swaying delicate motion of yesterday lured
me into the yes of when. this genuine delight of
shade, those enveloping eyes that open to night
gestures we never thought hung around in the
periphery of touch. the secrets told, the rumors
proven true, the sheep not sheep at all, but goats
that leapt cold heights and knew all along the site of
the lake. we were mistaken by anguish languishing
in the sun along the shore of your wound. they
stitched that long ago yet it bleeds its own secrets
while the considerate wipe away the red like any
book read before bed. the gesture meagerly suffices.
body parts, always body parts. our certainty knows
no limits in doubt. breezes blow in unobstructed.
loss of meaning, temptation, increase and freeze,
never the always of a wave bordered by walls. tiny,
frigid, penetrating, forceful, none of them all. how
can the miserly diminish the fueled fool receiving
awards for mistakes and childish reasons as reasons
for the squeamish lot. they cut trees park levels all
in the name of maturity. we, too, are mistaken.
you, too, as myself take too readily the hard front of
foraging the most delicate whispers. only moments,
only sun with thigh, flight with ear, your fright as
another affront against my best wishes. we deceive
as they never would but believed possible as a
marketing ploy. they receive as we never did but
wanted. how can they release when letting go is a

constant wound opening into joy and a spiral of
confusing clarity.

46

ache calcifies stubbornness in high chair, in seated
stool for mules of reasonably. the squelch nears
sameness bargaining tools in the shed, changing
mid-direction. optimistic. seasonally deranged
affected disorder. who hasn't. believe me. prepos-
terous signs declare what's right and wronged as
wrath of godlessness. blood begins to flow, oxygen-
ating awake like a tube fueled quibble.

quivering. a pulse. too many insects. embrace. i
kneel before you as queen to her subjects objecting
to all the kings men and whoever rolls over upside
turvy and squeamish misplacement of peas with the
mashed population of infinite mulberries and pre-
sent shortly, care to have a seat in the waiting no
room for me. i kneel but this bent haven of obsequi-
ous warnings, rash storm warmth, gales the force of
a gale forcing doors and windows opening into the
center of the lemon pit pale and sour. bit, bale, and
blower. i relent into deep gesticulation, in kneeling
at your mercilessness, at your kind of smile that
betrays weariness and insomnia the likes of which,
the dislikes of which, the spice that eliminates salt
due to high blood pleasure. is this supposed to be as
when here now, secrets bold face lie beside my
stupor, this lethargic head awake by day kneeling
toward ground zero. rip open my cord, let me drop

from the high chair mighty throne of encumbrance.
i might have thrown a fit, might have fit a throwable
pillow, a hugable disease that unrelenting stubble
pricks while seeming oh so sanguine. breathe me
you our welcome exile from this perjury, these
goose bumps, this premature engine groaning,
kneeling, and toppling over.

47

inside obvious places between the book ending
before the last paradigm. outside the oblivious
spaces beneath the hook sinking into the swimmer's
elbow and the vast see you later. these places look,
create, insinuate a self, incriminate others into
dramas scripted in languages misunderstood. a
crimean mystery play. an algebraic equation. a
symptom of obstinacy, preferably without wrinkles
and pass the ketchup, please. underneath the top get
to the bottom in this scurvy topsy delete the un-
printable mutilation masking silence as its cousin.
beneath my dignity. over my headache. i am besides
myself, inside out, crawling like a bottom feeder, a
mollusk, a must make way to the surface, to the out
door adventure, the swing arching higher than the
rested from a good night's sleep. pillow that punc-
tilious gift from salt please sandy shores and uncer-
tainty speaks wisdom in its own tongue.

i too yo we. spee lef as a fragmented caricature.
insipid nomenclature. my elbow joins with your
horrid malignity. make nice. make me vomit.

inside the breathe inside the nothingness of every-
thing placed in no particular semblance of disorder
shelved. inside the breath breathes ease comfort
sleep moan alongside between these branching arms
these changing remarks. breath inside nothingness
where everything moans in delighted ecstasy and
sun glows in damp shade and restorative poses
dissolve into a dream. inside wear out. inside the
out of hand out of mind out of breath. the inner
recesses the sideways stretches the smile breaking
surface skinny. in as egress or aggressive and wrap-
ping bamboo poles stuck in earth. i grow mourn-
fully dolorous in this evaluative twist, a vine climb-
ing into a descent of gravitational pulling elsewhere.
if this is ecstasy, give me a banana. if this is septem-
ber, remember the forgotten ambush, the snows
flurrying, the baseball flying. if between us is noth-
ing everywhere comes closer then faraway. the
distance unbearably between breathing amply as a
crop ready for cutting, a net ready for rolling, a tent
flapping in winded. inside my reach is another
stretch. inside your stretch reaching toward me
beneath towers of desire the dungeons of inhibition.
with such closed hands who can say how breath
moves. with such bold stands how can saying reach
anywhere other than a faraway intimacy along the
shores of another's delight. if this is the horizon how
seemingly rectangular. my breath inside yours
softens in the glisten of wet lips and earth saturated
with a light foot and sigh.

perpendicular hands in their peculiar positions
smoothed out the lair. my tongue coils in the slick
of reserved spaces

to do as not selfish or shells flung across the beach
doing as seeing fit as frightening as tighten your
belted. to do as not yes in the fresh morning do it
now whenever's okay buy me a brand new generic
holiday from extreme displeasures and soured
milking it for the last joke. doing as a yes as a dong
ding okay in the morning before the wee reaches of
light stream coffee brew and bedside manners with
bleached belches and pillows flung across your
roommate. doing as crossing sideways slipped
bedwise or sleep ignorant and raving past dawning
on me. having be do or us as them together in
solitary confined to closeted desires reeking havoc
on delights of breath easy on the cream and sugar.
being be as against the main stream mainly scream-
ing for ice cold colas or dystopian leaps across the
street of want ads and deleted memories reflecting
forward in an untoward fashionably crisply ironed
shirt sleeve.

doing as none other. ding dong as a mah jong game
no one kills. dung the dimly lit room the slightly
fitted blouse, every ounce cuts slivers and slices
fleshly spirited tales. do it now as yesterday fails the
test of tomorrow and who can wait their turning
back. by midday all evening gestures and middling
ways break waves break faster than saying the

alphabet in ideographic skits. whenever. whenever as now gets back to the turn of century phrased in a bent stemming from invisible sources, an underwater spring of fall. so often inflatable dreams race towards the tomorrow of then before anyone can play and remember forgetting as a civic mission or afternoon's entertainment in the cinema of a reach we as never before the moment which passed before our eye wear and oh so worn out. my pleas go unheard and your voice in the noisy silence amid parroted masses. that unity, the coincidence of flesh between matter and water over the grime of done ding doing what other's suppose like a stilled walking stick. how much more

surrender until squeezed as pinch of salt. my silence is unseemly.

50

effort

less

i think

no body's

thought

less

effort

51

coming as nothing before. in the reach of your palm my majesty beckons. if being so lightly as your skin brushing against my glance let being have it done with integrity and candle wax dripping. i as never always want don't the blush of rushing in pace when flames rise soft as burn. my cheek grazes your hush. your seeing approaches my resistance to falling timbers and crusted grass. i can reach no further without your stretch coming as nothing before this moment passing into the bliss of your attention. listen to the croak and hoot. simplify as thrust toward tissue and bone. my loss gains on my. my speech muffles noise of trying. as nothing before ever had me. as before when the plain spoken no shouted from porch and no touch left, no woody support or breeze softening. drip. words melt in nestled dreams too early to rise and bend their hands to clarity.

52

lizard face red and my bed rest failed the grimmest hope of plain facing off toward your gentle smoldering kin which remembers the bravest of the brave. these hopes as never always before beneath the cot and couched potato with math and speculation as an afternoon's entertainment amazingly so. the tv remote remotely reminds the unwind it in a hurry blurry girl. by breath of stubbornness and generosity of frank expression, as in give me your hand,

remove shoes at the door, and speak with an elo-
quence never used as mum. can we be brief. can we
abbreviate the private glance that grazes the sluice. i
give in. yield to the midas touch. whatever my
tools.

to have courage as say you love me i love who. the
meek will inhibit the wound as saying of sorting
through and sort of cute. half brave half timid as a
third going further ungirded. as say i love who hates
besides themselves slapped repeatedly across the
cheek of no smile. not able to finish as was started in
the middle. i can never. i always try. if you were.
belief fades like a withered balloon and the cut off
and the hole poked through you stupid, stupid. i
whom loved sneak peak thought the key hold this.
we can not easily rent this flat if flung open too
wide and privacy is adored by none. love has bal-
looned into hot air nobody loves meagerly or wisely
and between rarely speaks. the courageous love to.
the staged play of unreasonable. my own heart calls
to synonymously and silence answers to disbelief.
the unmade bed rolls doubt away and spills towels
to the floored desire, root and twine marry in a
disservice yet applause muffles the cynics sitting
timidly. it comes through. i aim to pleasure's mine.
stroke the cold fire flaming in memory. mute as
lamb's wool left unraveled, burned as waste not
want. belief is enough is enough. the sound is the
fury and blame riddles responsibility. i am left cold
in this passage. my book opens to my closure. your
pages turn me on. read this textual revelation, these
tentacles that wind tighter than a bed tuck. left

alone in the abandon of a moment's forgetting and, worse yet, ignoring the fact altogether. am i supposed to forgive and love and whimsical bicycle. but this matter draft supposes other's know is precisely the inaccurate vagueness that mass media applauds. your pleasure my anguish, my late night moans your noise ignored as mere background, as felt fabric of historical inadequacies and studies not learned. i lean in this direction, glare in the blur, blind in the amazing, the listen to what's not said and done again and again. oh say, it's not so and so. say it's i love you again and gain for fit and fancy like willow trees whose branches sway and know pliancy a snow fall and melt away hard knotty wooden legs. dream as knowing before and remember who loves what grieves for your buried self tortured by frozen dreams, stolen hopes and dismissals. wood rots, glass shatters, and seeds nestle while the brave feel the fellow and frighten the lazy and bench press pressure on the heart. i cannot know. knowing pursues me with its wish to impregnate and intercept with contraries, my own lax attempts to touch hold release keep current, keep mementoes and arm the leg of this journey to say with tenderness that horrors are just horrors, the pleasure mine coming to a home near you, nearby, lullaby.

hello is always an arm's length away, welcome as an ancient voice, a mythic wind clearing away, fertilizing, leaving the alone alone. together loves pursuit relentlessly. per chance.

just because others flew off the hand me down
doesn't mean mean you having it also. how much
attention is warranted by a five year or longer
guarantee sent in, cut at the dotted line up. just
because they trip you on the playground, flip you
the bird call, lip service a disservice doesn't mean
mean people. but if you want yourself wholesomely
refitted and reformatted to disk drawn high speed
knowing with a surreptitious smile and closeted
cloaks and remainders on the side walk, come with
me. calm issues forth from my own burn and scar
tissue. wandering minstrels and droplets of express
my innermost outgrowths as woven sweaters for
warmth and cold outrage. these meek markings
embolden the coy as urine in the snow and mark my
words as a smoldering spoken. i ask your forgive-
ness, demand you don't neglect, don't feign didn't
see, ears in perceptual harmony. string this along in
the key of a private delight stored in the top drawer
beneath socks and our glory. pay attention to free
attention. everything is for an unthinkable purpose.

54

the loosening. the goose neck bent to the steam and
snap snap snap as breadth of being. the splayed legs
and elegant feathers whether or not high clouds
striate muscles and minute particulars. as bible or
koran or torah. as the boring or the torn or the
coarse. as sublime as a light switch infinite of re-

cesses in the gray matter or the *prima materia* or what's that filament or illuminative glee. body me, oh buddha. wine me and die in your arms or ram it down your thrown away, trashed, like asking for forgiveness and getting guilt. loosen that tie if you will. lose that strap and scream. rap about it write in cursive incursion of doubt flying a fancy, tying a knot, slicing beef, and cut at the neck, what the heckle. register this. cash it in. what's your rate of return. turn around time in break neck speed. ring around the rosary and don't count your chickens before they snatch sense and whiff it or toss it like a wiffle ball waffles for break neck speed. as a pain in my need. the butt of your judgment divides, rips blossoms in break, break, break it ugly. take this not as formal complaint, unregistered and unofficial or suitable for those under thirteen overreaching or simply in the haste of speed and slope of slow. my responsibility ends with my reservations. your responsibility begins with your peculiar twisted tangle that toys with extremes between us. we are forever missing the point, lingering with doubt, shading the blaze and show me some of myself in glimpses of your hands around mine. i confess to knowing nothing about the criminal mention of a foolish heart and waves good bye. i confess to your crimes which insinuate collusion and slipping. we're in this together, two-headed and forthcoming. the strain of it all. the striation in ground dug for slugs and slug me one, will you, and cut off my necking in the back seat and poisonous slithering snakes and rosy bedlam and buddha's delight as christmas, christmas everyone.

like far. like creamsicle. like palatial. like lick, lick,
lick, sneak in the obsequious look. look at the
broken twig. cry out with sly wanderings and
wonder lust, wonder listing on a deep curve, a
driven coarse with nature unreserved and speak
your mine, always mine, gift wrapped preferred.
like closer and closure in infinite ways to name a
bloom and throw trivial concerns to water flaws and
wash in waters for shedding skins and sequined
rehearsals beginning always at sunrise. snap shut and
open wide. look both ways and divine. snap, pop,
and crack up, especially when down, especially
when higher than dragging shoes, unmentionable
pardons, and search lights that find stars, not the
gun. shot from the hills and hot for lingering shad-
ows revealing prompts and ploys in unrivaled
motion and leaps. waiting instruction. wading
through the muck and snafus of threads, drips, and
sultry breezes.

56

where the bright sky. where the opening opens less
by degrees. where sky bright not blight of fright but
a frequency that pitches balls and stitches mend and
rice paddies invite and not sequester, not set apart.
where the light sky, the night flying past as a dream
of presence and glorious vanities finally shelved like
a family memento, photo of presence without
abscess. where light whose sleeve dampens with

tears mend in a unity of fabrics and unraveling comes together in bliss in breeze in stars within view. where if not here. hear it or wear out its welcome, feet wiped across the material world, forgetting spirit, ignoring yaks and unicorns, my claps and your applauding ripped seams, as seems to be sew. if it fits wear it out in the eve of daydream. if it flies away then follow until pursuit of paradise or paris, whichever is reachable or wantable, too big for the shelving of possibilities into imposters of hopes. the vast open, the vase filled with water as clear as ocean before pollute, as transparent as mind before diffuse and deference to play or whatever rhymes with stay put in your seat, settle down, stick up for your shelf. widen to extremes of strato-spheric glee or, if dizzied by air, then ground, ground, down to florida or lavender or whatever makes scents and remembers body caught in corpo-ral mess divining, or can be, if need be, if we bend with time, if we send by degrees by dream and see what is needed, what bleeds, and what by twist of vein relates to us, ready or not, here it comes, plum in the middle, spine, breath, and pleasurably hum the sum or rub your tummy, lounge in the hot tub, tepid in time, fire it up all fiery, and ready to streak across the sky, comet, not comatose, nose high, not spirits low, open like a yawn, wide like an ocean, embraced as hand in hand for the band to play on and on.

if as when is a celebrate, then the light streams and
wanting is a legend's pastime. *ipso facto* or *ipsissima
verba*, ring, ring the new year or dangle earrings or
glide smoothly past the past and leave for compost
or a composition and suppose i don't and you do or
saying is as doing doesn't and remaining is frequent.
then drop the draw a string. then go jump in the
like you very much, love even or not at all, but to
please welcome into the house of dreams where
reality needs no disguise but drinks daiquiris with
abandon, loses tongues, and fills the sink with many
a dirty dish, cleaner than clean and leaning on the
coffee table, whoopee as someone didn't say but
heard it from the grappling few, the sap as sticky as
my cup of delight. as when is a celebration, then
fanciful dress softens touch so voluminously that
bats radar catch the blip and oh so, oh so, and here
we all go, and no, oh no, other than yoko and
hashito and me, too, me too as yippee and other
vernacular phrases that no one clips for her wall or
mirror or computer standard but widens the smile
and child's delight and oh so, oh so.

to plunge into waters fully breathing. sacramental.
ritual of sacred entry. how do i how do i am. be-
lieve it possible. believe in possibility. breath the
possibility not as fume but as per chance and heaven
scent, a message, a wise one, a ton of fun and sing

upon the wing of delight. my refrain. my para-
phrase, parachute, and unparalyzed fear of plung-
ing, the dive, or worse, pulled under, pulled under
breathless plunge, head strong and body suspended,
under water, under wasting time, beyond polluted
thoughts, and fish, fish, fish not for more but for the
nutritive now, generic staple. mouth open, bubbles
blown, pulled under by weight of body, by waiting
for want of better, for waning on the shore of
succumbing, knees bent, needs yielded, yellow
signals flash, flash, flash amid the quiver and quake.

now as snow drift, as sifting through ambitious pulls
away, put away, put down, reductive, read my
mind, read my liberation, rent your constraints and
run down the hill to sure, sure, sure as up the hill
and back down. the way of swings, the sway of see
and seeing, teeter tottering and spot check, spot
check and give it all up, crateful of thoughts, bagged
ideas, and bring me, bring me an abrogation, a
surrogate, the *axis mundi*, the syrup of knowing, the
breath of sun with glow of positioning possibility in
a kiln of kindred spirits taking form. speak this easy
as a peck-n-paw and bubbled depth, the silt of
lounging in the swim with desire, breath, and rise of
bodies grasping each other, clasping flesh in bound-
less ease.

59

in sepia rich soil, an image dissolves while i in
another dimension suspended between school and

locked out, strangled and estranged from rules that ripped scores and snarled potential. in sepia rich soil sprouts ouch, get off my foot and widely high and highly respected tumbles down somersaults landing in sepia rich toil accepting foot and weight, toots and horns, hates and delights in songs unaccompanied by violin yet mesmerizing just the same, the sane as different from me as you as plummeting down soaring up in the between of shadows and bag ladies and gentlemen seated in their tied up morality. earth calls like ravenous ravens and all the rage raving lunacy waving goodbye to hello and *hasta luego, senor y senoritas.* sonorous walks passing time just to pass the time of dumbfoolery. in every breath a passion wanes and births, in every breath, an awareness fades, in fashion and out, impeccably dressed and add money, a squirt of honey, and stirred passions rise up and dissolve, blended dull, lent like a bull horn or bullfinch if we dress in sepia, if we undress to sepia, if we as you never again but always this burn in the chill, always this still in the swirl calling as earth shakes and rattled window shades and come off it, come on to you, bless their heart, blessed art.

60

disembodying, lost self truncating desire forfeit and drag on my belch on curbed urges when seems dissolve in sand and dust covers my lips seeking yours, oh agony, oh leftovers of yesterday's vomit. mine as we recall the nascent swim. how can i. how in the distant reality, vague notions and stretch reaching to invisible closure opening arms like a baby's cry in the crib in the delivery making room for me. i sag under the weight of gravity and my own grave tendencies for open hands and your shouts, slaps, and unwritten histories, but bleeding on the carpet and dinner table. have a little respect. have a little soup. have it as i cannot until you but me in the line in the crescent by the half moon and above board overwrought with this steady gaze and wind blown desire, oh desire, and this unmade bed waiting your impress weight on my skin, bone, and moist between the sheets and the ocean's float welcome as never before but always sequenced while letting go the rot and stink and blossoms and fertile requests that render easy, that surrender this bride groomed for dusk dawn dreaming shadows that call like whispered music.

61

words escape my bliss bless you my son and daughters of the confederacy, words break open mid sentence mid phrase like a fruit ripped to its seed. no subject is too far fetch me my coat.

with eyes in the fire with stars in the commonplace with the without streaming as breath in the blue green atmosphere of this here and don't sleep as purposefully as bent at the needs cry out, coalesce, devour with sight in the fire. when bliss reaches as tickle as stand closer to reach the touch seek entry through the back door and front me one, will you, or back out of my your living sleepily and lazily under the tree and cross the field of my dreams. when we run away towards you. when we hold the sun in the palms of our handouts. when before is tomorrow's dream and yesterday a fragment of your usual drift off to sleep. my eyes gaze yours as slender stems and blossoms despite heavy handed tight banded and all the rock and rolling pins and king fishers and comeuppance, what a downer. drown me in the elegance of shattered dams to devour the knotty and the sleek. lucid in this confusion, i step madly wildly passive in activity, blind in the site seeing tour guide ungirdled and uncorsetted billowing flesh express knowing no restraint, a torrent of being as be and be and be. shaken to the crust as must be this fiery gaze and touch with your sharp claws maul tenderness as brightly as the strip of release. so often i say cannot when knowing is another story, a glory remembered, recalled, restored, rendered, refused, reused and rrrrrr as roaring. speak to me in your unspeakable language and sequester me as they and them and wrap the vine in me around yours boundless rushing water. i am saturated. lost. in the whirl of moats must should not and can. roll up sleeves to pull down ease. suppose as bookishly as a paint brush and stroke. i am breaking a mess heading straight for the curved road. i have given myself away as a presentable package never unwrapped placed closeted and remaindered oh so fond.

62

how false and obtuse. how strange and correctable.
how incorrigibly crafty. how now breezy clown.
stop now plow foul. say ouch when mean and more
when flowering essences. say outa here when come
again. stay away with the door open and flee quickly
to quicken processes in an eggful fertile spoke. how
dirt and deliberate in the white shadows of showing
off. how dreadfully deleterious in spinal fluid and
fingers tipping scales. hail to the cheer leader and
the boo hoo-er. how pale the chubby footed and
mass meanderers and problem as a stop. cannot
ropes me in. cannot blows the tires. what fire and
what light. what lighted friend forgoes homecoming
slender waisted and fill er up. divorce is never a
crying game but a forfeiture of love. never a unity
of opposites but oppose forced into situations of
take the house, leave me the honesty. separated at
birth and joined by the hippies. the cannot claims
my life but how else in the mastery of graveyards
shining lights upward bound plainly in the beckon-
ing of sweater and slacks, hilary and jack be nimble,
jack be get it over and done.

63

i do not wish to know as this seeing holds vastness
close to ribs and pleads forgiveness. i wish knowing
everything as glibly unsettled in the torrent of
tearful frightful flurries of creative impulses. my
flight knows no forgiveness and desire breaks open

to unwind to surrender the iron rungs and lungs that yield to breath. drowned in the sorrow of joy floating in airtight hope of hopelessness. my wings contradict the feat of everyday's launch and cliff climbers tumbling sideswiping and nearly missing. i cannot say what hasn't come forth. belief is the moon's shadow on the street, walked on, run over without a flinch or slow down. i cannot say what grieves in the dark recesses or on the playground of the grim and open chested. such treasure chests without keys so break in break up and break pining for what's not here or dear or feared as flight or pray and jangled jewels and glittering eyes beyond what's dreamt and lied upon like a rug woven in blood and breath, floods and death. i cannot say what they died for, what strives for up or down, pointed exactly to center creeping crawly.

i wish knowing this seedling open, this entelechy like a sentence written across my flesh with periodic pauses for traveling to river's surety in a moment. i wish knowing as a blown feather and lavender inhaled full of blended sorrows and a grin that knows no remorse. like a galloping steed or an errant duck. like a ring around my finger and your blouse untucked. to sigh in such relief of hold me tighter in your arms to share the wealth that craves morning's light and moon's beam. no holding back without letting go on and on. no scolding no matter the vulgarity or crayons smashed or shorts torn. no blowing away what's meant as beginning in the dawn of remembering. these fingers know only branches. these toes know only earth and sun, sky

and by and by for those who rest in the brilliant
caress of blistering ease, the twirled canvas, and the
play as a hop, skip, and glee.

64

i am listening the only way i know. i call you
through partial numbness in attempt to escape my
attempt for fully found, no fooling or following
false leads and leaden games that striate skin and
clog arteries. i call you other than me but the same
nonsense in the eve of dusk might i offer an opinion
free of pining and ringing chimes. i'm appalled by
this lack of feel, this apathy that circles playgrounds
without every playmate running away. this circle
connotes a decided turn of phrase and twisted
phalanx and the sun always rises no matter how
often it settles down. but settling down never is but
rounding planet but astounding this crowning
achievement as a continuous stream knowing no
end only constant motion. bare all because stand
this numbness. bare all because landed gentry and
feminine wiles have lost ground and blood spatters
freely throughout suburbia.

65

the why of because no longer concerns ambushes
and blushes by extremes. because shy blushes why
here not as a sidestep dropping out to drop in
dripping wet. the why exercises distaste that, like

rotten fruit, reeks of overspent and waits too long.

into the watering pool. into the why of because. into the pool ocean sliding reason away slipping on slippery rocks washed ashore away from surety. deep in the depths of extremes immeasurable beyond yard stick and quantum leaps from high dive unsuitable to flesh and pinched thighs. if giving in is a why of because then so be them that they inside this house home barnyard fielding dreams corn my husk and know what must be done. in the apple of my eying the pit of believability doubt souring sweetness maturely like a well rounded point and a pen knowing only flow.

to unteach ourselves we unyarn the ravel, spill forth gutterally and climb on bars like a child's musing. to unteach ourselves, we unyard the gravel, spill forth gutterally and roll marbles along the flooring you with expressed differences and simultaneous excla-mations of gosh, geez and oh my belittle your grand neurotic demise that takes hostages pilgriming in the pillage of once upon delight.

the why of cause and effecting me as nothing that came before slipping on banana peels and bathing in a hot tub all afternoon with slender legs dipping out and sugar for all.

if i step outside myself and go inside where the air is more shall i say shall i say do you want me to stay do you want me to help in the kitchen though i don't want to help in the kitchen though i need help you're not giving though i gave at the office though you stayed at the office past dinner and i shall stay in this spot to comment on all that's not right with this table and chair hair splitting coughs and conjunctions that know no pause and excuse me whenever. if i may grab a moment to steer you in my direction if i may linger where the fire roars and glows my spiritual longings and why is it that we listen to the snout of reason, not the irrepressible queen of imagination and lock our daughters in their rooms and insist our boys play in the street where they cut up frogs.

if i as you in extremes of displeasure and remarkable goodness of purity of being having been doing dong again in the simplicity of the difficult remarkable silence that deafens and blinds and helps in getting home away from this pine of flesh so uncontainable in this continental drift. i say together as shy not because the only reason saying all in the duff is enough is enough.

if we were to let blend into an emaciated glory that radiates sublime letting glow and grow. my own critical faculties would be sentenced to hard laborious plays without scripture. what our eyes cannot see our ears suspect. that faint whimper. that puppet of pleasure and hedonistic exile.

listening as body feeds for fuel and foolish diatribes crossing fields with streams of behaviors skipping into frolic of girlhood and other dark hoods alighting her step and skipping in step to drum, peel, and breath. as body needs blood the breath the listen of writhing desire that won't away wantonly in kali games. body bloods the breath and eases the scream delicately whispers its wants and glistens with fullness as empty as sea-free sea shells. breath listens to lists and drift, weds names that branch or craft careless devotion caretaking giving everything away, all trundle beds, all blouses, every ounce of strength, every louse and friend in neighborly picnic in the mass gravity. as feed for friendship in bitter sweetness rotating doors of hellos and sorries, those worrisome apologies forgotten glories that pass with breath into dust. as bodily as a sinking craft in waves of extremes and drifting thought about you the other day. drifting thumbs tap tables for charitable glances that don't register as anything other than an unregistered other.

body sifting and perceiving, listen, smote, take away, give up, remove every cloth, every barricaded word, every sigh that dismisses, every log that jam jam jam. lifting and remove the offal, messages in bottled up and unshattered, ships that anchor to port of call, call to prattle, tattle on and titled in impressed wood, not by less and more current streams. every sigh, no mourn, every die, no life, every morning with breakfast in bed and blankets covering fleshscapes where wilder than easy trembles with invisible invitations. this torture of release, this realization of the empty shell formed by ocean, spit by pull and toss, held by opening, given breath, sand, revolving in the drift of attentive hands.

67

die to the moment's glories and rewards, stream line unlines to unnerve this being that was and is always never the same. i die in this wake. cry out to crayons. they could never be as they are. cold nerve ending sleep in the forest. i get stopped. released to the grandeur of nothing, no boxes with jewels, no mailed checks, no announcements that proclaim a proclamation. so insidious.

should i be looking at what i want. should i be. i shouldn't be anything. dissolution like evaporated rain, like pain numbed by pill, like knife in throat. a thoraxic grid. i succumb to my own failure. desire is my undoing. i collapse onto bed to roll into the ocean to drown. in yielding to pressures larger than my smallness, my quintessential nature, my insect status, as low as economic depression and despising for squish. i follow the collapse and surrender. i lose to they and the we that rarely enters the door with recognizable gifts. in my pain is my end and my beginning if resuscitation is possible, plausible, positive and internment camps far from this city. i know the pricey jewels. i sowed the reaps and leaped the warnings. i forget the learnings and lean east desiring a longer braid. in the belly in the tongue. in the belly in the tongue. the heart of the mat. the heart of the dream that awakens the sleeper with fits and stares into rooms with no closed windows curtaining the world. i open the drown of blessed irreverence shouting profanities at doomed malls and values that don't fit the tolls. i run from the hide and seek me out. i sleep in the daze of twisted ruse. i rise with breath that dies with wind and sun, slipping on ease, struggling with rocky ledge and swimming mightily to sure or habitual desire. i cut out this heart on paper dissolving in the dispersion of happenstance and never-mind.

68

outside this inside. the tent canvas. he leaps across boundaries. she stretches her contraction. they meet nowhere in the distance. touch elbows and nod agreement that they abandon themselves, dissolve into the desert, blend with horizon, prone themselves, display the invisible. they agree and walk away from the remoteness for an intimate coupling, a doubling of singularity, sensations that toss words useless. sound only for ground this orbit of chills and heat. they glance at nothing and shriek delight. they lose themselves in erasure, in dilution, in twists and chants and impregnable imaginings. they leave never having arrived, they come never having gone, they repeat what they haven't begun. and try again. always trying again. to unravel strictures tied to job, house, and conventions that threaten to strangle. they disappear. they reappear. flickers in the light. sparks amid the fire. splashes in the wave. in a glance, a graze, a caress, an indifference, flesh matters, vessels uncontainable, boats willing to sink, children uneasy in maturity. whether the desert calls or voices a whine, they uncouple, divide, the sum not equal to parting, the departure of rare meeting, the unfelt fleeing the felt diction of touch, sand and bitter wind, land and take off.

69

his my. the wetness of dry. the tension in tenacity and release of braided hair. we wept. we lingered in shadow to no longer conceal the hidden, to voice the forgotten and muted, to unravel the twine. her my. the moisture of heat. the ease of giving in, giving away, surrendering every last first, each middle and final start, cotton and suede, shouts whispering misgivings, the caress of yes. we plummeted, fell from the highest peaking, sinking into the deepest feel as casting out, net again, to outlive the habitual burn, the scar that refuses, the toppled tree. he tipped me a twenty dollar bill. she bullied him with kindness. they yinned and yanged, zipped and zoomed, hippity hoppity how. oh, shekinah of delight, oh buddha body, oh twirled dervish. we as they devour the caress and light up the moon. they as we slice pieces into fragments to make whole holy. who can believe such deceptions when stream rants otherwise in weedy glory, in needless desire of restless sleep and dreaming awake. our we. they together it alone. slam softly into hope and bounce off wailing the unspeakable mention, pardon me who is her to him against the wail sleeping in bedlam and peace. i greet you in farewell. you goodbye to returning and leave impressions, residual sounds, echoes, vibrations that color these pages and maintain the want of earthsky oceanrest.

70

she who removes veils spells words.

she who knows past present slides her legs across your horizon. she who slithers to shed skinny meets the between whenever possible for infinite trespasses beyond. she who doubts ruins reputations with praise. she who climbs trunks packs bags in a moment's notice this

asks questions and believes.

71

beside me beside you bedside. blessed with bliss of blood flooding desire. flavored for taste for touch for the linger of fulfill. tender away from don't, tempting to do. flying beside you, falling between us. doubly scored and indubitably bitten, giving up what underscores welcome bliss, the kiss of light shedding skin. outside me you inside you. graced with glance of ephemeral tug, whistle, and whole. placed where one aught, where two might, where three struggles release. a galloping foresight, a dazzling delay, an incursion of presence that neither foil nor unfulfill.

bones separate from tissue, wander no further. ruptures wave farewell to mend ways, amended texts, disclosed secrets, frayed nerves, and loose threads. always seeming what is and more. always believing less but more. her body shifts, loosens chains and remove. his embodiment loosens tie, lessens pain, and flings.

in the slow music of spheres. in the slack tension in the tepid air of ease. mold knows only cold. breath wants open, bones unblemished, blood coursing in the bedside between us in the besides ourselves the slow grow of coupling dissolve.

72

he that hows. she that speaks. that move between whispers. that slip between sheets. that lumbar rolling. that tongue coiling. this diachronic end with synchronic ring of awake. she who is never. he who was once. they who become we. the us of centuries. the selective tribe remotely touching, see-sawing and he-sheing. cursed with this blessing. grateful for the hurt. woe to be gone again settled along the river's side in the openness of distance.

i don't want. i don't wanna. i don't wanna be the
queen's bee, the eaves of eye, the crave of sore, the
wound of the bound unwinding down, finding the
soft spot, spot checking, signed check, hairy
chested, bald or bland, band-aging and aching for
what's no longer apparent or wheeled in the car-
riage by the mother tongue or father desertion. i
don't wanna sleep. don't wanna weep. don't wanna
say what's not to be said, what's not to be had or
dreamed or mimeographed for class. how honey
and molasses. how sunny delight in ignorance of
massive factors, population out of control, media
carelessly mediating without a lengthy meditation
on the caress of breath. take it away, take it away,
take it away, i say. give it away, give to they, live on
to play the games of adore, sure and furious
schemes whose outcomes go out with the trash and
in with the shiny. to want one's mamma or want
one's dada after something romantic, candle light,
candle bright, a drama of glory.

what i want what i want. what want is not to want.
what wail in legendry application to the crass. in a
snail's pace along the path to grandeur and supply
without demand. if this is cage, then argue for
release. is this is stage, then demand rewrite. is this
is rant, then dive to the bottom of pooled desires
hiding in underwater cravings. is this is is, then what
a want, want an ant's perspective, what a stepped
on and pressure lifted.

you irremissible enslaver of benign identification.
you smelly rose of rotten rotunda. you armpit of
footfall in the fleet of night. you awakened be-
moaner of abandonment. you broken splint of
banners, burnt toast of side dish. you gallant gal-
loper tripping on hippydom. you insipid swine cast
as castaway. you homing pigeon. you flatulent
billowing breezeway. you artificial stanza of unpat-
terned disarray. you bonkidity bonk and diddity-
doo who never did and never will. you scraping
moronic seismic encounter. you seizure and clo-
sure. you taker and leftover. you molecular blot ink
dribble. you papryian summary of nondisclosure.
you contracted virus of stingy grandiosity. you
beeswax and ant dung. you mind your own business
and sleep all day. you egg roll and half eaten pep-
peroni. you philosopher. you speech queasy not.
you ephemeral scratch and sideways glance. you
whimsical musical refrain. you undotted i. you
drawn outside the lines and insider of the beltway.
you ungrateful belly. you legend brewing in your
own tribe. you criminal of love. you dadaist play-
ground. you dreamless vision. you polygraphic
homily. you parsimonious broccoli stalk. you
vegetarian. you dystopian. you leader of the will
and won't. you bore me. you bother me. you
parentally disgruntle me. you dote on me. you
smote and i might. i smoke and you blow me away.
i am wind to your ways, heat to your ice, shine to
your blindness, and i'm still listening.

so long in the distant of far. so nearly here. so long
in the distant of far nearly here and missing pieces
fragmented by quakes. distant in the far nearly
missing figments of imagining. so far in the near
miss imagine this in the long draft of short cut and
cut off mid-sentence. so short in the mid-section
and bare mid-drift increasing distance between high
and low cursory devices that devastate soil. in my so
drift and journeying banter whispers the imagined
soil of brain teased explanation seeds breaking
surface. so surfaced in the nearly broken sentence
removed by far closeness at break neck speed and
arm's lengthy reach. in nearly reachable shouts of
joy and more deliberate displays guaranteed by
chance. as a decoy of coy pursuits given by gen-
dered rules of ladylike which bugs the hell, pardon
my frank belch express pressing me in shoved up
against your face it.

i am not far in the closed-minded clothes lined for
drying and inked possibilities beyond engendering.
sometimes i mow the yawn and sometimes i poke
the halibut intestinally. but reachable derivatives of
unusual events happen standing along the waiting
wall, the wailing wall waiting, so it seems, to
pounce into opportunities open handed or closed
fistula. merrily we go away to remain as close as
immediately announceable. this whispered soil
tracks my steps. these impressions hold preter-
naturally in unspoken unsentenced crossroads. so
long in the crossed trodden down. so near in deci-

sion's directions pointing this way best over thata-
way or a more zenographic route. i camp in the
rootless microbic earth that chews and churns.
more than stone in shoe. more than fly in soap.
more than you take the high road and i take what's
left brained. assert to assist. nearly missed is nearly
gained in the game of foul play. desist what destroys
or destroy entirety to revive sprouts of companion-
able thoughts and acts carried past intersecting
impossibilities. watch the listen to feel the broken
mend. fold the map to unravel the dream. so nearly
in the future of the back foregrounded in shadows.
so close in light turned bright star and sun in eyes.
rolled out dreams unfold the unmapable impalpably
but with imaginative certainty. like a road signing
off. like a treaty of inverse. like a vest unbuttoned
to cotton of nearby field, nearby stream, formal
opportunities in bloom or rush openly spaced apart
in a united front.

76

where i go when i stay. whenever i stay put down
and put away. wherever i never go away for stamen
and pistol fire. i never make statements that dis-
tance the diastolic pulse. i every instant distant static
hyperbolically with a heroic welcome and putdown.
whenever insults happen, stay awake. wherever
inversions convert, create a wake of unreasonable
applause and pretend the stool flipped. stay wher-
ever you aren't. stay awake with the blink of an
aerosol spray. spray away the unintuited dementia

welcoming stray beasts and broken dreams. stay
where stray away. say way out and over here and
whassa matter, didn't say, didn't do, not yet i
betcha. go way away from shore and swim away in
place as play in heat sun beat burn stream lingering
hoopla. circle three times. spiral as fast as position-
ing regardless of point or sandy tracks. spin in
unlimited abilities like tree hopping or smashing
mashed potatoes. who knows how the starch boils
to size. who shows the stretched barbed wire. i
never sit when i stand up. i never lie on the truth,
unless sand bagged or feeling down. i never swim in
a reclining chair, set low, set for towing the wiles
away. gives me the willies. gives me a head attack, a
knack for strain in plain aggrandizement wherever
preferring to swing from the tree on an unobligated
tire. rest easily in the stay away, blessedly stated,
the lesser of two evenings, the devil made me
drowsy, the snitch caught my draft and laughed me
away uneasily.

77

duly forgotten gathered together in the here and
nod off, we have lathered here on this most lubri-
cated of days to grieve. oh warrant of daisies, oh
wearying begonias and bygones, garnished with rose
petals detailing the lingering staff influence.

78

she could not pretend. pretensions dissolved in the grass, ground to dirt. she could not contain the tensions, apprehensive masks ripped off, shattered in the thrust. desire not deserted, having not for hire, not for rent or twisted out of lineage or acred hopes. leaping over misgivings, clawing at questions refusing to give answers, paths that know no toppled tree too high, boulder block and might not. fierce roaring hilarity, ferocious frenetic pounce, kinetic bounty. boldness unbound, unchecked hat at the door, rain or saliva, potential bursts on the scenery, the greenery, ferns and grips ripped flesh wounding the right claim, the mighty take, bargain or whole salvation.

emerald eyed myriad sighted blind to none spoken up and none in complainer's finery. emerald eyes seize all mouthed and tongued. untied lapping ungrappled prayers. plea for none please. pleased by acquainted. tainted by pretensions but masquerading as torn, bloodied, tried body taken by haul to stream the marked glory gratified by absolute pulse and breath, pulse and bedded desire ripped into wrapped unraveling skin.

79

let go. let glow in the glib privacy of your humble attention tuned obliviously to obviate mistakes of identification plastic or myelinated. let flow in the

flowering essence of stumbling deficiencies ob-
structing instructions instinctively vectoring starry
eyed eclipses. shadow me in adumbrated guises,
lies, and leave yourself beneath the tree, stumped
on folly. if you trumpet for me i'll foot the building.
if you toot your harangue, i'll hang my shins at your
dreaded bereavement, tomb that leaves no room to
sweep clean, to weep as witness to cringing. no
remorse here. no memory either. no second guesses
that puzzles irony and flattens the swell folks. in
light of low blight on characterizing me an assump-
tion of glibness or women's libations. no hindrance
here. no mnemonic devices either. just slow gyrated
grabs and tuck, rolled with a buttering up.